Some kids are into sports. Other kids know all about dogs or trains. Not me. I love science! Recently, I have been studying sunsets. Today, my friend Sal and I swam in the lake. Later, we watched the sunset. It was beautiful. I wrote down the time in my science notebook.

Sunset Times:
Tuesday: 7.39
Wednesday: 7.38
Thursday: 7.37
Friday: 7.35
Saturday: 7.34

"The sun is setting earlier every day," Sal said.

"That's because the season is changing," I said. "Summer is almost over. Autumn will be here soon, and then winter."

"I get it," Sal said. "In summer we have long days. But during winter, days are short." Sal thought for a second and then grinned. "We'd better get ready for snow," he said.

"Not yet!" I said.

4

"Remember my pen pal, Mateo, from Argentina?" asked Sal. "Well, he said they got some snow today. I bet it's heading our way."

"Wow," I said. I shivered in my swimsuit. "I do NOT want snow today!"

"We'd better go and change into some warm clothes," joked Sal.

"Don't worry," I said. "We won't get snow tonight." I shivered again. "But we do need to go back to my house. Let's go!"

We went to my flat. Sal dug out some winter clothes. My dad helped me find a website that shows temperatures all over the world. We found Mateo's city in Argentina. Argentina is in the Southern Hemisphere. We live in the Northern Hemisphere.

Next we looked for Mateo's city on the globe.

Sal pointed to Argentina on the globe. "So, is it winter in the Southern Hemisphere right now?"

"Eureka! Yes, it is!" I said. Eureka is a scientific word. I use it when I get excited about a new discovery.

I jotted down some notes in my notebook.

Seasons in the Northern and Southern Hemispheres happen at opposite times. When it's summer in the Northern Hemisphere, it's winter in the Southern Hemisphere.

"Let's think," I said. "What makes it warm on Earth?"

"The Sun," replied Sal.

"Eureka! That's true!" I said. "And it says here that the Earth has an axis. It's an imaginary pole that runs from top to bottom through the Earth's centre."

"That makes sense," said Sal.

← Earth's axis

"The Earth spins, or rotates, on its axis. It moves around, or orbits, the Sun at the same time," I said. "It's amazing that we're not dizzy!" joked Sal.

Earth rotates once in 24 hours. That's why a day on Earth is 24 hours.

"Let's try something," I said to Sal as I walked over to the globe in the corner. I grabbed a small lamp and removed its shade.

"Let's say this lamp is the Sun," I said.

The lamp shone a bright warm spot on the top half of the globe. "That half is the Northern Hemisphere," I said. "The light shining on the bottom half, or the Southern Hemisphere, is more spread out. It's not as strong."

Northern Hemisphere

Southern Hemisphere

"OK," said Sal.

"As the Earth rotates, part of it is pointed towards the Sun. The other part of the Earth is pointed away from the Sun," I told Sal.

"But that doesn't explain why weather changes," said Sal, "or why snow is coming."

"Snow isn't coming!" I said.

While the Earth rotates, part of it is pointed directly at the Sun. That part of the Earth experiences daytime. The part of the Earth pointed away from the Sun is in darkness. It is nighttime there.

I spun the globe around again. "Because of the Earth's tilt, the Northern Hemisphere is getting sunshine longer than the Southern Hemisphere. That means the day is shorter in the south."

"Always?" asked Sal.

"It can't be always," I said. "Because we know our days are getting shorter now, at the end of our summer."

"Maybe the Earth changes the direction it is tilted," said Sal.

Dad sat down and joined us. "Earth's axis is always tilted in the same direction," he said.

"So how does the weather change?" I asked.

"Remember, the Earth also moves around the Sun," he said. "In fact, it takes one year for it to go around the Sun once."

"Eureka! That's right!" I cheered.

"I get it," Sal said. "It's winter in the top half of Earth when more light is shining on the bottom half."

I picked up the globe and walked around the lamp. Soon, more of its light was shining on the top half the globe.

"And it's summer in the top half when the Earth is over here," I said. "Now more light is shining on the Northern Hemisphere."

Seasonal changes happen because of the Earth's tilt on its axis and its orbit around the Sun.

I moved the globe around the lamp to see how the light changed. "Areas near the equator get lots of sunlight all year," I said. "As the Earth orbits the Sun, the amount of sunlight doesn't change much there. The weather doesn't change much either."

"Okay, but what about areas near the top and bottom of the Earth?" asked Sal.

"You mean North and South Poles?" I replied. "Near the poles, the amount of sunlight changes a lot. The North Pole gets six months of sunlight during the summer. The South Pole is in darkness all that time. In the winter, the North Pole is in darkness for about 11 weeks in a row."

"That's a big difference!" Sal said.

"Yes, it is!" I said. "Let me write this down."

Places near the Earth's equator receive a lot of sunlight. So areas near the equator don't have as many seasonal changes as areas further away from the equator.

North
Pole

Equator

South Pole

Dad's phone rang, so he walked out of the room. Sal grabbed a coat and put it on. But soon his face was getting red. He must have been getting sweaty in his hat, gloves and coat. He said, "So Earth moves around the Sun once every year. It's always the same."

"Yes, and we can predict when the seasons will change," I said.

"I predict it will not snow tonight," Sal said.

"I predict you are right!" I replied.

The change in seasons affects people, plants and animals. Farmers know the best time to grow different crops. Some animals, such as hedgehogs, hibernate during winter. Some animals migrate, or move to different areas, to find food or shelter.

The next afternoon, Sal and I went swimming in the lake again. Later we looked at my science notebook. Sal guessed the Sun would set at 7.33 p.m. He was right!

"Still no snow," I said.

"Thank goodness!" Sal said. "I'm going for another swim. Will you take a picture? I want to e-mail it to Mateo. He won't believe I'm swimming in the middle of his snowstorm!"

Tuesday: 7.39
Wednesday: 7.38
Thursday: 7.37
Friday: 7.35
Saturday: 7.34
Sunday: ??

When and where does the Sun rise?

The Earth orbits the Sun. As it does, daylight changes with the seasons. Get up before sunrise one morning to learn how daylight changes in your area. Don't forget to bring a pad of paper and a pencil.

1. With an adult, find an open area like a beach or large field. Write down what time the Sun rises. Take notes about what you see*. Draw the eastern and western horizons. Put a mark to show where the sun rose.

2. That night, go to the same place to see the sunset. Take notes again about what you see. Put a mark on your diagram showing exactly where the Sun went down.

3. Repeat the activity about three months later. In your notes, write about any changes you notice. Why do you think there were changes?

*Be careful not to look directly at the Sun.

GLOSSARY

equator imaginary line around the middle of the Earth; it divides the Northern and Southern Hemispheres

eureka cry of joy or satisfaction

hibernate spend winter in a deep sleep; animals hibernate to survive low temperatures and a lack of food

Northern Hemisphere the half of Earth's land and water surfaces that are north of the equator

North Pole the northern-most point on Earth; the North Pole is in the Arctic

orbit travel around an object in space; an orbit is also the path an object follows while circling an object in space

predict say what you think will happen in the future

Southern Hemisphere the half of Earth's land and water surfaces that are south of the equator

South Pole the southernmost point on Earth; the South Pole is in Antarctica

temperature measure of how hot or cold something is

READ MORE

Seasons (Ways Into Science), Peter Riley (Franklin Watts, 2016)

Weather and Seasons (Popcorn: Science Corner), Alice Harman (Wayland, 2014)

WEBSITES

http://www.bbc.co.uk/guides/zcx3gk7
This site explains the different seasons.

http://www.bbc.co.uk/bitesize/ks3/science/environment_
earth_universe/astronomy_space/revision/5/
This site explains the reason for seasons on Earth.

COMPREHENSION QUESTIONS

How would life on Earth be different if the planet was not tilted?

The Sun gives us light and heat. How do changes in light and heat affect plants and animals?

Because we know about the Earth's tilt and orbit, we can predict when seasons will change. How might this be helpful? What would happen if seasons changed without warning?

MORE BOOKS IN THE SERIES

INDEX

Raintree is an imprint of Capstone Global Library Limited, a company incorporated in England and Wales having its registered office at 264 Banbury Road, Oxford, OX2 7DY – Registered company number: 6695582

www.raintree.co.uk
myorders@raintree.co.uk

Text © Capstone Global Library Limited 2018
The moral rights of the proprietor have been asserted.

Edited by Shelly Lyons
Designed by Ted Williams
Art Director: Nathan Gassman
Production by Katy LaVigne
Printed and bound in China

ISBN 978 1 4747 4051 7
21 20 19 18 17
10 9 8 7 6 5 4 3 2 1

British Library Cataloguing in Publication Data
A full catalogue record for this book is available from the British Library.

Acknowledgements
We would like to thank Christopher T Ruhland, PhD, for his invaluable help in the preparation of this book.

The illustrations in this book were digitally produced.

Every effort has been made to contact copyright holders of material reproduced in this book. Any omissions will be rectified in subsequent printings if notice is given to the publisher.

All the Internet addresses (URLs) given in this book were valid at the time of going to press. However, due to the dynamic nature of the Internet, some addresses may have changed, or sites may have changed or ceased to exist since publication. While the author and publisher regret any inconvenience this may cause readers, no responsibility for any such changes can be accepted by either the author or the publisher.